INSPIRATIONAL
Book
of POETRY
and READINGS

INSPIRATIONAL
Book
of POETRY
and READINGS

JOCE ROGERS SMITH

XULON PRESS

Preface

I have always loved reading poetry, verses that rhyme. I can remember reciting poems for special occasions at a little country church in Chapel Hill, North Carolina. I was six or seven years old. My mother, from time to time, would have me recite those poems for her friends during visits with them. I did as any six- or seven-year-old would do when asked to "show off" a God-given gift or talent. I did it reluctantly. Mom was always proud of those presentations, nonetheless.

Over the years, I never lost my love for poetry. I took a poetry class as an elective in high school. That class eventually opened the door for me to read various poems during the morning announcements. I felt special. During my teenage years, my love for reading and reciting poetry continued, and it was then that I began to write poetry. I was active in my local church in Miami, Florida; therefore, I was privileged to share my love for poetry at special occasion programs and events. One's talent and gifts make room for themselves, as Scripture states.

This book does not contain all of the poetry that I have written over my lifespan. Some of my writings reflect times and situations that are too personal to share. I get solace, though, when reading my "private" poems. Some of them remind me of the difficulties of life, such as disappointment, betrayal, naiveite, and loss. I cherish those "private" poems because they reveal what it means to survive. And then I am reminded to appreciate the determined, confident, and strong black woman God has blessed me to become.

This book is dedicated to my husband, Pastor John Thomas Smith, of forty-eight wonderful years of marriage. Also, this book is dedicated to my children. They are the three heartbeats that I am so humbly proud of: John Thomas II, a high school physical education instructor; Jeanette Marcelle, an elementary education teacher and music instructor; and Jason Terrance, a recent 2020 recipient of his Juris Doctorate Degree. Presently, he is a Mayor's Aide in the county mayor's office. I also dedicate this book to my beautiful grandchildren: Jaylah, Jason II, Isaiah, Leilani, and Lana. Lastly, I dedicate this book to the cherished memory of my grandson Jelani, who is resting in the arms of God. A previous book, *Memories of My Grandson, Jelani Teriq Bryant,* was published following his transition in 2015.

I pray this book will live up to the title and be an inspiration to the reader. Some of these writings are a direct reflection of the times we are living in. Some writings reflect the harsh reality of this day. All of these writings will express my faith in a sovereign God, who sees all, knows all, and cares.

POEMS TO BLESS YOU

I See God

I saw God this morning when the sun rays filled my room.
I saw God when the rain fell and drenched the ground at noon.
I saw God in the evening time when the sun began to set and hide away its shine.
I saw God when the wind swirled up the leaves, and they ranged my wind chimes.

If you look, you will see God in everything you learn.
His love and grace are for everyone, even those who can't discern.
If you pray, you will feel God, no matter what you face.
If you believe, you will experience God's love and His amazing grace.

Stop, turn around, take a look around and see.
God is holding the earth in the midst of the sea.
Turn around and smell the roses, as the birds swoop up above.
He lets the sunshine in and the rain fall down, just to prove His love.

Just look, behold the earth's beauty that's all around.
The white mountain tops, the green valley low in the ground.
By God's design, the rainbow glows and the snowflakes fall.
So, slow down and take a look around; God is the creator of it all.

Then your light will break forth like the dawn, and your healing will quickly appear, then your righteousness will go before you, and the glory of the Lord will be your rear guard (Isa. 58:8 NIV).

Missing You

Some mother, father, sister, brother, or child has crossed that great divide.
While they are absent from our earth, they are resting at the Savior's side.
We say their names and think sweet thoughts of them, for sure, each day.
Yet they are missed, no matter what, but here on earth we're bound to stay.

We say their name from time to time; it stays there in our hearts.
They are missed and forever remembered, but they were summoned to depart.
Our loved ones are angels now and are up there around God's throne.
Not missing us we know, for they are up in heaven, and peacefully they are at home.

Their beautiful souls are whole, not broken or bruised, and totally free from pain.
As promised in God's Word, peace, rest, and a crown of jewels they now can claim.
We are loving you, as we are missing you, although God is the only one who knows.
So, we will call your name, over and over again, until it echoes within our souls.

One day, and it will be a glorious day, when we shall be with each other once again.

We'll be rejoicing and shouting and singing with God! Oh, the joy will never end.

Until then, we will walk in hope, and we will live in peace that God's will is perfectly done.

Those beautiful memories will be held close, as we thank God for a life that was well run.

Lift up your eyes and look to the heavens: who created all these? He who brings out the starry host one by one and calls forth each of them by name. Because of his power and mighty strength, not one of them is missing (Isa. 40:26 NIV).

A Family in Love

There is nothing on earth dearer than a loving family.
The family, a close-knit unit where love flows full and free.
Good morning and good night begin and end the days.
The family cherishes, and holds close, those old familiar ways.

Love is the bond for keeping each family member in place.
Prayer is the key; it turns strife and descensions away.
The family, oh so dear to God, is designed by Him alone.
His earth was freely given to man, for the family to make a home.

The God-fearing family will make Him the center of everything.
By honoring God with the first fruits, more blessings He will bring.
Seek Him daily for wisdom; it will guide your family each day.
Then trust and rest in Him, as your family loves, laughs, and prays.

For the sake of my family and friends I will say, "Peace be within you" (Psalms 122:8 NIV).

Precious Union of Husband and Wife

When married, saying "I do" to each other is not the final end.
In a God-fearing marriage, each partner must hold on and contend.
Vowing "I do" can't fix the problems that loom or make them fade away.
Communication with God and each other will make love glow and stay.

A husband and wife must surrender, completely, to one another.
Love then can endure and flow freely as the marriage flourishes.
Hand in hand lovers must walk and push through obstacles of life.
The couple climbs mountains, endures valleys, but holds on in spite.

The love of a husband and wife is an unbreakable bond forever.
Sometimes turbulent winds may blow and cause them inclement weather.
Wrapped around God, and knitted as one, they can endure the raging sun.
A marriage with God as the head will stay weatherproofed, as one.

That is why a man leaves his father and mother and is united to his wife, and they become one flesh (Gen. 2:24 NIV).

Equality and Love

All the people walking and crying for equality.
All the people are shouting for love and peace.
Our black brothers dying from brutality of bad police.
Our black sisters too are gunned down in defeat.

The world is full of people who just do not see!
This is not freedom for all, nor is it real equality.
Would you want your brother dying in the street?
Would you want your sister gunned down in defeat?

All the people must walk and cry out for equality.
All the people must hold their hands up for all the world to see.
All the people must demand justice as well as liberty.
All the world must walk and let love, instead of blood, spill out
in the streets.

Our desire is not that others might be relieved while you are hard pressed, but that there might be equality (2 Cor. 8:13 NIV).

Bad Policing

What will happen to my grandboys when they become of age?
Will they live to grow old, or will they get trapped by untrained
police rage?
Will police shootings stop before there is an incident with them?
Will the laws change to protect and defend their young innocence?

Hearts grow dark and heavy every time a black death is shown.
Though all lives matter, it's the black lives that receive unfair scorn.
Some are shot on the street, alone and unable to make it home.
Many tears fall down the cheek when those news clips are shown.

My black brothers, by adverse abuse, dying all alone.
Being choked on the street by insane police is just all wrong.
Over and over again this tragedy plays out, and again it is rerun,
Black brothers and sisters taken out by bad policing, hands,
knees, and guns.

I walk in the way of righteousness, along the path of justice (Prov. 8:20 NIV).

A Child's Decree

I want to be something great with the life God blessed me with.
Perhaps I can change the world by using my talents and gifts.
Maybe I can be a fireman and protect people from burning flames.
Perhaps I can be a good police and protect citizens from those
that harm.
Maybe I can be a lawyer and plead the cause for humanity.
Perhaps I can be a doctor that treats all kinds of disease.
Yes, I know being president is also a possibility.
With God's help, I can be just what I want to be.

I don't have to be rich to have and live out my dream.
I just need to imagine and keep God on my team.
If you teach me determination, I am sure to prevail.
I can then reach my full potential and set my ship to sail.

Start children off on the way they should go, and even when they are old they will not turn from it (Prov. 22:6 NIV).

This Season

This season is the time with family and friends we share.
Thoughts of love and good deeds go out to show how much we care.
The joy of this season is really caring for others in some small way.
A kind word, a prayer, or a smile can make some lonely person's day.

This is a season where peace, love, and joy should be truly genuine.
God has spread His hands and shared His universe with mankind.
Each person must reach out to touch someone else's loneliness,
While loving hearts and loving hands are busy showing tenderness.

God has ordained this season, a time for everything under the sun.
Blessings from God are plenteous, flowing freely to everyone.
Our Savior's gracious mercy lifts us up from defeat and gloom.
Let us praise Him for His greatness and in our hearts give Him room.

He made the moon to mark the seasons,
and the sun knows when to go down
(Psalms 104:19 NIV).

Faith

Longsuffering goes hand in hand with peace.
So, give your troubles to God; He will grant release.
Hold on; stay strong; your suffering won't last long.
God will lift your burden and let your heart sing songs.

Gentleness is what you'll need to deal with life's low blows.
Don't be dismayed, keep the faith, and watch your fruit grow.
Goodness and faith are the makings of a Godly, holy life.
No matter what you see others do, don't be the cause of strife.

Your belief and faith in God should be nothing new.
It is faith and confidence in God that will see you through.
Rest in God; wait for Him; on your behalf, He'll move.
Follow His Word; it's your guide, and your pathway will be smooth.

They must keep hold of the deep truths of the faith with a clear conscience (1 Tim. 3:9 NIV).

Just Pray

When you're feeling glad, and your heart has a song – pray.
When you're feeling low, and your troubles are strong – pray.
If there's a void in your life – pray.
If you are confronted with envy and strife – pray.

Life is full of ups and downs, long, winding trails with ins and outs.
Give your problems to the Lord; through prayer He can solve them, no doubt.
It's true, you should know by now, that prayer will certainly change things.
So, pray on, saints, ask what you want, and see your prayer take on wings.

Prayer reaches to the heart where troubles lie and brings deliverance to the troubled soul.
When you are down – pray; let God straighten things out and loosen the heavy load.
When you are up – pray; tell God how grateful you are for His awesome joy divine.
When life is really good – you better pray, because God is the one that makes your sunshine.

Prayer will soothe the heart and chase all your blues and troubles away.
You must hold on for another day, lift up your head, and continue to pray.

Morning comes after the long, dark night, and our God is not deaf, I know.
Believe in Him while you ask in faith, and watch Him give the devil a final blow!

Is anyone among you in trouble? Let him pray. Is anyone happy? Let him sing songs of praise (James 5:3 NIV).

What Time Is It?

This is the season for love and good cheer.
This is the season to look forward to year after year.
This is the time we look to receive in large magnitude,
But this should be the time we thank God for His blessings untold.

Our Lord Jesus Christ is the reason for this blessed season.
His immaculate birth brought us new hope beyond reason.
Oh, feel the joy of our Lord's merciful, redemptive love.
It is most precious and showered from heaven above.

Thinking of God's love should bring you great cheer.
So, be glad when you give and share gifts this time of year.
This is the time to worship and praise God as we celebrate,
But remember, He wants a place in your heart before it is too late.

And God said, "Let there be lights in the vault of the sky to separate the day from the night, and let them serve as signs to mark sacred times, and days and years" (Gen. 1:14 NIV).

Christian Brothers and Sisters United

Christian brothers and sisters are united in prayer and praise.
Together, we sing the praises of God, who is perfect in all His ways.
We will stand in awe of His greatness as we reference His great name.
We are working together in love, not for selfish motives or gain.

The sun is set in a magnificent sky, then turns and goes away.
Stars shine for His majesty, and they bow, they swoop, and they sway.
We must hallow His precious name and give glory to the Lord above,
Through prayer, faith, and praise; He will cover us with His blood.

Christian brothers and sisters united can withstand any storm.
We can be like the rock of Gibraltar as we hold up each other's arm.
Christian brothers and sisters, stand united with power from above.
Nothing is impossible for us to do with God's help, His strength, and His love.

Christian brothers and sisters, look up as our joined hands are raised.
Our awesome God will establish our path if we bow in prayer and praise.
Therefore, don't faint, don't fight, don't let go of His loving hands.
Christian brothers and sisters, go forth as we lean on Christ and stand.

And over all these virtues put on love, which binds them all together in perfect unity (Col. 3:14 NIV).

Meekness

Meekness is not weakness, as some may have thought.
Meekness is the fortitude to be kind and humble, even if your
effort seems for naught.

Meekness is taking down when you know you're right.
Saints do it for peace's sake, to avoid a fight.

Meekness lets the other person go ahead and have it their way.
That's because Saints know, in the end, our Holy God will pay.

Go ahead, put on some meekness; heap it up real high,
because it's no telling what you will face before the day goes by.

When Satan throws his darts, don't fuss and don't fight,
because the meekness of God in you will bring you out alright!

But the meek will inherit the land and enjoy peace and prosperity (Psalms 37:11 NIV).

Sing Praises

When troubles come and your spirits are low,
Sing praises to God until your spirit soar.
When friends are few and loved ones gone,
Sing praises to God all day long.

When seeking answers to your worst fears,
Sing praises to God as your answer nears.
Singing praises to God will make troubles fly,
sooth the wounded soul, and dry the teary eyes.

Don't you let troubles and doubts stop your praise.
Trust in God and let Him direct all your ways.
Sing praises to the God no matter what you go through.
Sing praises to God. Yes, God, I sing praises to You!

He says, "I will declare your name to my brothers and sisters; in the assembly I will sing your praises" (Heb. 2:12 NIV).

Love and Brotherhood

God commands us to love our sisters and our brothers.
We are to say kind words no matter if they are brown, white,
black, or other.

We all must pray for peace in this, our sacred land,
Then pull each other up so that each one can firmly stand.

Racism, killing, and violence mocks the love of God for this world.
Hatred, vile pride, and harsh words will not move the world onward.

Love, justice, equality, and peace is what the masses need.
This will come for sure when Christians stand and bow down on
their knees.

For this is the message you heard from the beginning: we should love one another (1 John 3:11 NIV).

An Immigrant's Decree: Let Me Stay

I came here with nothing.
You took me in,
Lonely, lost, and afraid.
I thought we were friends.
But you sent me back, again.

My strength was gone.
I couldn't breathe.
You rescued me.
I didn't freeze.

Lost shoes, clothes, the ring.
No voice, no song, I couldn't sing.
My legs are short, my feet swell.
The wind blows hot; it's an awful smell.

Tomorrow's promises, not gone yet.
If you leave me be, I won't go back.
It's here and now, I wish to be.
I want freedom, work, love, joy, victory.

And you are to love those who are foreigners, for you yourselves were foreigners in Egypt (Deut. 10:19 NIV).

Mother Taught Me

She loved life, so with faith in God, she did all she could do.
She gave of her time and of herself, for me and others too.
Mother raised eight precious hearts and lifted them to the sky.
She refused to give up on us when trouble lingered neigh.

Mother left something behind for sure; this we all know.
It is a legacy, a dream, and a purpose for eight heart beats to grow.
What could be so great, as our memories carry us back far,
As to see mother working, pulling, and pushing us up to the stars.

I must go forward, keep the faith, and plod on no matter the cause.
I will face my tomorrows with vigor, purpose, and hope
without pause.
There is no looking back for me, nor do I have a fear of the unknown.
Mother taught me well, so I stand on her shoulder of prayers
and press on.

From birth I have relied on you; you brought me forth from my mother's womb. I will ever praise you (Psalm 71:6 NIV).

His Soul's Delight

Oh, how I wish that I could see my mother now.
In a long white robe, she would be singing in the choir.
She would be wearing golden slippers on the streets of gold.
She would be prancing and dancing, never, ever to grow old.

Lord, You must know the pain in being left behind.
You must have a reason for picking flowers that are mine.
No, I don't understand what You feel or what You know,
But I rest assured You'll hold me near until it's my time to go.

Dear Lord, calm the aching hearts as You lighten the heavy loads.
Give peaceful rest to the weary minds, let sorrows be no more.
I want to see her and tell her, "All is well; rest and sleep tight."
But Lord, I will not go to her, until I am Your soul's delight.

They entered into a covenant to seek the Lord, the God of their ancestors, with all their heart and soul (2 Chron. 15:2 NIV).

God's Colors

Brown, black, and white, dark and light,
Not the colors of the rainbow but the colors of life.
Souls woven together through the world of work and play.

Night and day, democracy and justice ring their bells.
God guides the colors along a winding road; they turn and swirl.
Colors rub together in a world of work and play.

The colors flow to an end in the valley below,
While waiting for the sun to shine and glow.
Hope is present, love also, as the colors work together and play.

Love does no harm to a neighbor. Therefore love is the fulfillment of the law (Rom. 13:10 NIV).

WELCOME ADDRESSES AND SPECIAL OCCASIONS

The Welcome Word

Welcome is a word that should come from the heart.
It should sooth one's soul right from the start.

A welcome should put the stranger at rest,
Make a sad heart merry, and then let the host be blessed.

Welcome is what you say to a friend when you open your heart
and you let them in.
Welcome is how you show your care to a visitor, loved one, or a
comrade friend.

So, to each of you who have, gallantly gathered here with us today,
I offer this very special word, "welcome," glad you came, hope
you enjoy your stay.

Today we will share hospitality and warmth, throughout the day,
till the end.
So now we say welcome to each of you; our sisters, our brothers,
our friends!

We will be sure to treat you with love so grand,
So that you will be happy to come visit with us again!

Welcome!

*Anyone who welcomes you welcomes
me, and anyone who welcomes me
welcomes the one who sent me (Matt.
10:40 NIV).*

Welcome into This Place

Welcome into this place!
Greetings in the name of our Lord and Savior Jesus Christ.
On behalf of our honoree, and the rest of our honored guests,
I bid you a warm and heartfelt welcome to this eminent occasion.

May the songs you hear inspire you.
May the fellowship you receive reacquaint you.
And may the delicious food you eat refuel you.
Welcome, welcome, welcome into this place!

Welcome into this place!
It's designed by God to reflect His grace.
Welcome into this place!
Our hearts are aglow as we look upon Your loving face.
Welcome, welcome, welcome into this place!

Now when Jesus returned, a crowd wel-
comed him, for they were all expecting
him (Luke 8:40 NIV).

Welcome to Our Service

Good evening and welcome! Your presence is a pleasure for sure.
So, as we celebrate our church today, we also celebrate you.
God has been graciously kind and good to our church family, year after year.
And because you came to be with us today, your love for us is ever so clear.

So welcome! We are very glad to see you this evening.
Now I would like for you to help me welcome the people sitting around you.
Will you touch three people and say, "Welcome, I'm glad you came."
If you are bold enough, just ask, "What is your name?"

Oh, you did just great! And with that said, let me explain,
May you feel more blest when you leave this place, than when you came.
So welcome! We pray you enjoy the service, and we hope you will come back again!
Welcome!

So, he came down at once and welcomed him gladly (Luke 19:6 NIV).

Welcome Greeting

Greetings to each of you in the name of our Lord and Savior dear.
We honor you today, and we are glad that you are here.

You are welcome here, where we have worship services throughout
the years.
You are welcome here, where we praise God each Sunday morning
with jubilant cheer.

You are welcome to this place, where the Word of God is preached
continuously.
It is our pastor, a servant-leader for God, who has a vision for
this ministry.

You are welcome to help us promote that vision until it comes
to fruition.
So, welcome on behalf of our pastor, his wife, and the members
of this congregation.

Welcome, welcome, welcome to each of you, I say.
We feel so blessed that you have come to fellowship with us today.

May a song from the choir lift you,
May the word of God make you feel renewed.

May you leave here today rejoicing as you go.
Be blessed, saints and friends; we love you more than you
will know!

Welcome! Welcome!
We speak peace over you the more!

But the crowds learned about it and followed him. He welcomed them and spoke to them about the kingdom of God, and healed those who needed healing (Luke 9:11 NIV)

Welcome to Our Celebration

Good evening to all of you, our distinguished guests, friends, and saints.

I officially welcome you to this wonderful occasion that nothing can outrank.

It is indeed a pleasure to have you join us for this glorious celebration.

Now you may wonder in your mind, what exactly are they celebrating?

We are celebrating the awesome power of God that has sustained year after year.

We are celebrating the wisdom of God that has been our guide without fear.

We are celebrating the love of God that has been our motivator to just stand fast.

So, we stand unmovable on the Word of God because what He says will last.

With the help of our almighty God, and your prayers and your support,

We can press on to higher heights and deeper depths in the Lord.

So welcome, help us lift up our Savior's name as we thank Him for one more year.

Welcome, saints and friends! We are so glad you came, and we are so glad that you are here!

Welcome!

When they came to Jerusalem, they were welcomed by the church and the apostles and elders, to whom they reported everything God had done through him (Acts 15:4 NIV).

Welcome, God Bless You

Thank you for coming out to be a part of this celebration.
You didn't have to come, we know, but we are so glad you did.
Your presence means so much that we want to show you appreciation.
The program was designed with you in mind, our family, our guests, and friends.

Welcome to worship in here, and help us set a spirit-filled atmosphere.
Join in as we jubilantly sing praises to God and usher His spirit in.
The choir, the ushers, and the members here, will show you that we care.
We thank God that you joined us today, our loving family, and our friends.

Welcome, perhaps the prayer will cover some need you have.
A song, I pray, will bring some joy today, and tomorrow too.
You'll be encouraged, we pray, by the preached word that's shared.
Welcome, we speak peace to you as we say, may God bless each of you!

Welcome!

When he arrived in Galilee, the Galileans welcomed him. They had seen all that he had done in Jerusalem at the Passover Festival, for they also had been there (John 4:45 NIV).

Jesus Loves Me and You!

Jesus loves me and Jesus loves you.
He died on the cross, so I know it is true.
But don't be sad; Jesus rose from the dead,
And He is our Savior, just like the Bible said.

Jesus loved us from before time began.
All we have to do is to take His hand.
He will carry us throughout the heat of our day.
We just need to talk to Him as we go our way.

Our Savior's love is steadfast and true.
From day to day, His love shines through.
No matter the trial, He is holding your hand.
Just lean on His shoulder; He is your friend.

Thank you for worshiping with us today.
You are welcome to enjoy the Lord in your own way.
It feels so good to have support of family and dear friends.
Welcome one, welcome all, please come back to our church again!

But I trust in your unfailing love, my heart rejoices in your salvation (Psalm 13:5 NIV).

Resurrection Welcome

Welcome and good morning to everyone that is here.
We celebrate the resurrection of our Lord, who is now forever near.
Just as we welcome you, Jesus Christ is also welcome here!

Today we bring a simple message to each and every one of you,
That Jesus died for the sins of the world, as He made all things new.
Behold the beauty of the earth, as only He can show!

Welcome to our celebration of our risen Lord and Savior.
May you be blessed today and every day with God's divine favors.
He wants to live in your heart forever and to be a present guide.
So, just hold His hand, follow His plan, and He will walk right
by your side.

Welcome one and all!

And who through the spirit of holiness was appointed the Son of God in power by his resurrection from the dead: Jesus Christ our Lord (Rom. 1:4 NIV).

INSPIRING THOUGHTS

QUALITY VERSUS QUANTITY

*I*n April, another birthday came and went. I became another year older. While it is definitely a blessing to be a year older, I noticed that I'm unable to do some of the things that I enjoyed doing in my younger years. For example, I have been sitting in my bedroom looking at a few stained spots on the wall. I would love to paint that wall. In fact, I would take pleasure in driving to Home Depot and taking my time to look at color charts to match the paint.

If, when I get home, the color swatch didn't match, I would enjoy hopping back up into my SUV and driving back to Home Depot, the same day, to get the correct color swatch. I would repeat that step until I matched the paint. After the match, I would head back to Home Depot to order my light-yellow paint. Then I would be so excited to paint when I get back home that I would charge into the project immediately. I would put the "hurt" on those marks on that wall, as we used to say.

I understand why it is important for individuals to commit their lives to Christ in their youth, as I did. It is evident that they will be able to do more for Him. They will be blessed with more stamina and can grow into the knowledge of Christ day after day. A young, committed Christian will be a great representative in the church, on all levels. They will also be proficient in their homes and community involvement and be competent on their secular job as well. I was.

I turned seventy years old in April and realized that I do not have the amount of stamina to work at a high-energy level in the various areas of my home, church, and community as I had, and did, in my younger years. I have, though, maintained my commitment to excellence in every area of my life. Although the quantity of what I do has decreased for sure, the quality has not.

Not just our work, but the quality of our work will speak for our tenacity as Christians even after we are gone. Therefore, the Christian should be concerned that their kingdom work be that of high quality versus low quality and high quantity. I believe the level of excellence in what we do, be it little or much, is a direct reflection on our commitment to our faith and the kingdom of God.

And whatever you do, whether in word or deed, do it all in the name of the Lord Jesus, giving thanks to God the Father through him (Col. 3:17 NIV).

Pray and Look for It

*A*re you looking for the thing to come which you asked God for? If not, it may be an indication that you don't believe God will grant your petition. We have to live out our prayers in expectancy. Christians do that, I believe, by feeling confident that what is asked of God will come to pass. Next, begin to look for the object of your prayers. A "living faith" is demonstrated by walking in expectation, not seeing it but expecting it by looking for it.

For instance, thirty-two years ago, I petitioned God for the home we now live in. It was a brand-new home. With my husband's blessings, it was 1987 when I started the search. I contacted a realtor to show us various properties. I looked at each piece of property in faith. Although it was an arduous process, for two years, I kept looking because, without a doubt, I believed God heard me.

I was confident that we would get the brand-new home. Confidence was there because: 1) my lifestyle was pleasing to God; 2) I fasted about the petition for the new home; and 3) I honored God with the fruit of my labor, tithes. I had fulfilled what God required of me, so boldly, I petitioned Him.

It took about two years before we found the house of "my" dreams, but it happened. We still occupy that home today. It has been the site for many blessed occasions, including children's graduations, high school and college. It has been a place where new babies (grandchildren) have been welcomed into the world. Retirees have been celebrated here. A mortgage was burned. Just as holidays and many other family milestones have been, jubilantly, celebrated here, loved ones have been publicly mourned with repasts here as well.

The "circle of life" has truly been experienced in this place. My husband, John and I, have been, and are still, so blessed here. This home is standing proof that when you petition God, believe God, then look for it to happen!

But you, when you pray, go into your room, and when you have shut your door, pray to your Father who is in the secret place; and your Father who sees in secret will reward you openly (Matt. 6:6 NKJV).

I Have My Umbrella

I didn't have a car when I first started to work in the professional world. I was right out of high school. So, I took the bus everywhere I needed to go. Public transportation was reliable, practical, and convenient. There was only one car in the family, and my mom used it to get to her job.

Rain was the biggest problem I can remember being faced with as I took the bus to and from work or to downtown shopping. It took me a short minute to realized I couldn't predict when it was going to rain. Plenty of mornings when I left home for the bus, the sun was shining bright. However, by the time I got to where I was going, rain would be pouring down. Hurriedly, I would exit the bus in the rain and find a building overhang for shelter.

In no time at all, I learned the value of carrying an umbrella everywhere I went. When clouds were out, the umbrella was by my side. It was the sunny days that fooled me. But I learned, even on a sunny day, rain clouds could appear from nowhere and flood the ground. I became quite a weather girl. Habitually, I carried an umbrella with me everywhere I went.

My spiritual journey reminds me of those days of my public transportation experience. The umbrella became a valuable tool that I had with me at all times. The Bible is that necessary tool that I have with me at all times. I never know when I will be confronted with disappointment, grief, or some other problem where I will need spiritual guidance.

Reading God's Word, the Bible, gives the Christian an edge. God's Word will give us direction to overcome obstacles in life, whether they come suddenly or otherwise. You may not be able to have the physical book with you at all times, but reading and studying the Word of God makes it real in your heart. You can carry it with you, in your heart, everywhere you go. The Word will be with you whenever you need it. Just as my umbrella was never out of reach when I took public transportation, God's Word will never be out of your reach as you go about your daily routine.

Your word is a lamp unto my feet and a light unto my pathway (Psalms 119:105 NKJV).

Laughter Is Like Medicine

I'm still amazed at God's great creation, the universe, and especially the creation of mankind. We were created in God's image, according to Scripture. God is love. He gave mankind the capacity to love also. God is kind. He gave mankind the capacity for kindness. Jesus wept. Mankind is able to weep when it is necessary, like Jesus did for His friend Lazarus.

I am amazed also by the fact that God gave mankind the gift of laughter. However, I have been unable to find documented scripture that suggests that Jesus laughed. Just as Jesus cried, I believe He laughed at some time during His earthly journey. Remember, He was human like us, but without sin.

We dare not believe that laughter was not an emotion, gifted to man by God. I have experienced the fact that laughing makes me feel lighthearted. There were times when I have faced gloomy situations, but being able to find something to laugh about decreased my weariness. Laughing didn't take the problem away. For some reason, though, laughing gave me a different perspective about that problem. Things were not as bad as they first appeared.

There is scripture in the book of Proverbs that tells us how good it feels to laugh. I believe we can be pious Christians and yet enjoy the emotion of laughter. My stress level decreases when I laugh. My perspective change when I laugh. Although Scripture does not state, "Jesus laughed," I can't help but think that God gets enjoyment when He sees me rack my side in laughter from time to time. Try it.

A merry heart doeth good like a medicine: but a broken spirit drieth the bones (Prov. 17:22 KJV).

We Have Limited Strength

We have limited strength. However, with the power of God working in and through us, there is no limit to what we can become, accomplish, endure, or achieve. Great men and women in the Bible demonstrate the power and strength of God in their lives.

King David would not have defeated the giant without the strength of God. Moses would not have successfully led the Hebrew children out of Egypt and across the Red Sea without the strength of God. Noah would not have been able to build a gigantic boat that saved his family and the animals of the earth during the great flood were it not for the strength of God.

When we give our life to Christ and put forth every effort to live for Him, then Christ gives us the ability to deal with all things that life may throw at us. Embarking upon a new chapter in our life could produce feelings of dread, apprehension, or even fear. Things like changing a career, pursuing an education, buying a new home, or even getting married for the first or second time could be cause for apprehension.

No matter the challenge before you, God will help you on your journey. Simply align your ambitions, dreams, and goals with the will of God. Consult God through sincere prayer. If need be, solicit the advice of Christians who care about your well-being. Next, proceed with confidence as you move forward with the might of God.

I can do all things through Christ who strengthens me. (Phil. 4:13 NKJV).

Together in Unity

We are all a part of the body of Christ, although we are all diverse and unique individuals. The minute we accept Christ as our Lord and Savior, we have joined ourselves to the body of Christ, the Christian faith, and family of believers. But we are different individuals with different gifts, talents, and abilities given to us by God. Because we are in Christ, our differences can be a blessing to the church and a positive influence on it. Souls will be blessed when different gifts, talents, and abilities operate in unity.

In fact, we ought to be glad to be a part of what's going on in the kingdom of God. Although we may differ in talents, spiritual gifts, and even opinions and ways of doing things, we can still be united in the spirit of unity. Operating in the spirit of unity means we will demonstrate a positive attitude at all times. Such an attitude creates the groundwork for successful accomplishments for the entire body of believers.

When we operate in the spirit of unity, we will support God-fearing leaders. Where there is no unity, there is no peace. Selfishness cannot abide where unity exists. Compromising one's own ideas in the spirit of unity may be necessary, at times, when working with others.

Unity should be apparent in our family interactions, between the husband and wife and between children and parents or guardians. Interpersonal relationships in our churches should be a demonstration of unity in action. The Christian can, and should, be the torch bearer of unity on secular jobs as well. Just know, something good is bound to happen when we allow the peace of God to govern our thoughts and our actions.

Just as the body is one and has many members, but all the members of that one body, being many, are one body, so also is Christ. (1 Cor. 12:12-13 NKJV).

What's Going Viral?

$\mathcal{A}$ few years ago, I taught a class at the community college where I retired. The class was called Office Procedures. Before the start of class, I would tell the students, "Please turn off your beepers." It sounds ancient, I know. However, this world was just on the verge of the electronic messaging explosion.

I think the most important chapter covered was where the text explained that a technology explosion was on the horizon. That chapter taught that the office professional should have and demonstrate integrity at all times. Further, it was explained that the office professional should not do anything at eight o'clock in the morning that they wouldn't want seen on the six o'clock evening news. This demonstrated how fast news would travel due to advancements in technology in the future.

A few years later, advancements in technology brought us instant messaging. It is a blessing. But it is vital for Christian women, men, boys, and girls to understand the importance of exhibiting Christian values when we text, tweet, use Facebook, chat online, make videos, and more. The list goes on and on.

When it comes to instant messaging, we should ask ourselves, "Does what I am about to send or post represent Christ?" Everyone must know of some embarrassing, unfortunate incident where a professional or a public figure lost their job or were ridiculed on the evening news because a tweet, text, or post mishap went viral.

We must think of instant messaging as our tongue by which we speak to express ourselves to others. Before pressing "send," examine if what is about to be sent is going to help or wound the receiving party in some way. Is it going to reflect the spirit of God that lives within? If you use electronic messaging to connect to others in a positive manner or to lift up and encourage others, then you are doing great ministry. Kudos, keep up the God work! If what you are sending will hurt, wound, embarrass, or tear down a person in any way, don't press "send."

A wholesome tongue is a tree of life, but perverseness in it breaks the spirit (Prov. 15:4 NKJV).

The Perfect Marriage

My husband and I have been married for forty-eight years, as of January 20, 2021. I enjoy reflecting on the early years with my soulmate. Some forty-eight years later, though, I have noticed something peculiar. Some of the differences we had in our early years are still with us today, at a lesser magnitude, of course.

True, some things have changed; we are both college educated and retired from professional careers. The children are all grown up, although not very far away (in shouting distance). We have grandchildren who are an intricate part of our lives. These are all wonderful changes. I am so very grateful that we have reached this milestone and season of our lives together.

Upon becoming a wife, though, I thought with age and maturity that our marriage would mellow and age to perfection. On the contrary. My husband and I still host marriage seminars; we are the special guest. We still have misunderstandings. We read from different pages of an issue. There is still a "pet peeve" list on the refrigerator. Some have taken the place of others.

Thank goodness, we no longer disagree over how to raise our children. Now, we disagree over how to steer the grands. There is a discussion if there's no gas in my car when he, randomly, gets in to drive it. Of course, he heads directly to the gas station. Mind you, he willingly gases up my car. I just forget to tell him when the tank is "almost empty"…well, "empty."

Yes, forty-eight years later, wiser and matured, we still have our differences. Years ago, I heard that "opposites attract." Would you believe my husband is a Leo and I am a Taurus? I am of the opinion now that we will always have our differences. But the best part is, we have maintained our faith in God. He is at the center of our marriage. Also, before I forget to mention it, we still cry when we are overwhelmed by goodness, or at the loss of loved ones and friends. We still laugh with each other and at our own mistakes and blunders, as well. All of which shows how human we are. Last but not least, we still love smoothing things over and making up no matter who is right or who is wrong. And I don't want that to change, ever.

Though one may be overpowered by another, two can withstand him. And a threefold cord is not quickly broken. (Eccles. 4:12 NKJV).

God Alone

A while ago, I had trouble setting up one of my notebook computers. It was small but as powerful as a desktop computer. I called the computer tech service line for assistance. Evidence of the times we are living in, I was talking to someone overseas, in China or Japan perhaps. I was amazed at the efficiency and cost effectiveness of such a process and procedure.

I am thankful and amazed at the vast amount of knowledge that God has given mankind. God has afforded man phenomenal knowledge, such that they are planning flights to the moon. In the future, you and I will be able to get on a flight to the moon just to get away for a time. In the future, if a person gets tired of a spouse or companion, they will be able to, literally, send them to the moon, as I've heard said before.

We are blessed with advancements in medicine and science. God has also blessed our nation to be one of wealth and prosperity. Therefore, we should remember to reference God and honor Him for how He has blessed us, individually and collectively. We are blessed in every area of your lives. Homes, vehicles, a job, and the provisions of life are all evidence of the love of God that is shown toward us.

We should give God credit for our prosperity, health, and our mental capacity as well. Sure, people immediately thank Him for things considered to be enormous blessings. But I have learned to give Him praise and gratitude for even the minute realities I experience in life as well. Christians in my denomination thank God for "life, health, and strength" on a daily basis. These things are priceless. God alone deserves the honor, praise, and glory for this. Why not give it to Him?

Give thanks to the God of heaven.
His love endures forever (Psalm
136:26 NKJV).

CPSIA information can be obtained
at www.ICGtesting.com
Printed in the USA
LVHW010403010821
694234LV00021B/1900

9 781662 818240